Weddings, Funerals and Dedications

Dr. Nathan Ogan

Providentia Books

March 12, 2011

First Printing: 2011

ISBN 978-1-365-19893-9

Nathan Ogan

This is a self-published book. Readers are invited to offer corrections for spelling, grammar and various other suggestions. Please submit any such corrections or comments to drnogan@gmail.com

TABLE OF CONTENTS

WEDDINGS IN THE BIBLE

A marriage ceremony with its accompanying activities is found in the New Testament in Luke's Gospel, 12:36 and 14:8. Among the Jewish people a wedding was a celebration in which the entire community was expected to participate. It would go something like this:

- When the wedding day arrived, the bride would put on white embroidered robes, along with jewels, with a fastened a bridal girdle around her waist, covering herself with a veil, topped with a garland on her head.
- The bridegroom, dressed in his best clothes, with a headdress, then set out for the house of the bride's parents.
- He was accompanied by friends, musicians and singers, and by persons carrying torches if at night.
- The bridegroom would receive his bride from her parents with their blessings and the good wishes of friends.
- He would lead the whole wedding party back to his own house or his father's house with singing, music, and dancing.
- On the way back they would be joined by other friends of the bride and groom.
- A meal was served and celebrated together.
- That the evening the bride would be escorted to the nuptial chamber (bedroom) by her parents, and the groom by his companions or the bride's parents.
- On the next day the celebration was resumed, continuing for as many as seven days.

Marriage in the Bible

Marriage was instituted by God when He declared, *"It is not good that man should be alone; I will make him a helper comparable to him"* Gen. 2:18. God fashioned the woman and brought her to the man. On seeing the woman, Adam said, *"This is now bone of my bones and flesh of my flesh; she shall be called Woman, because she was taken out of Man"* Gen. 2:23. This passage also emphasizes the truth that *"a man shall leave his father and mother and be joined to his wife, and they shall become one flesh"* Gen. 2:24. This suggests that God's ideal is for a man to be the husband of one wife and for the marriage to be permanent.

God's desire for His people was that they marry within the body of believers. The Mosaic Law clearly states that an Israelite was never to  marry a Canaanite because the Israelite would be constantly tempted to embrace the spouse's god as well Ex. 34:10-17; Deut. 7:3-4. This was the tragedy of Solomon's life later in Scripture. Likewise, the apostle Paul commanded the members of the church at Corinth, *"Do not be unequally yoked together with unbelievers"* 2 Cor. 6:14.

Although romance before marriage was not unknown in Old Testament times, it certainly played a minor role in the life of unwed partners of that era. They didn't marry the person they loved; they loved the mate they were married too. Love began at marriage, not marriage begat from a love relationship. When Isaac married Rebekah, the Bible records that *"she became his wife, and he loved her"* Gen. 24:67.

On one occasion, when Jesus was asked about marriage and divorce, He quoted two passages from

5

Genesis. *"Have you not read that He who made them at the beginning 'made them male and female,' and said, 'For this reason a man shall leave his father and mother and be joined to his wife, and the two shall become one flesh'? So then, they are no longer two but one flesh. Therefore, what God has joined together, let not man separate"* Gen. 1:27; 2:24; 5:2; Matt. 19:4-6. Jesus taught that marriage was the joining together of two people so they become *"one flesh."* Not only did God acknowledge the marriage; He also joined the couple.

Minister's and Wedding Ceremonies

When a couple approaches a minister about performing a wedding ceremony the following is good to keep in mind:

- While the minister decides who he'll marry or not, the church body has the right to decide what times are appropriate for use of the facilities. (See Application for Use of Facilities, Appendix A and Wedding Guidelines, Appendix B)

- Counseling prior to the ceremony is essential. My normal requirement is a minimum of two sessions, unless requested. (See initial evaluation form) In the case of under-aged minors, state approved counseling and hours may be required.

- Discuss arrangements prior to ceremony. (Announcements, invitations, etc.)

- Review vows

- Insure that couple has registered with state and is prepared to present the certificate for licensing the marriage on the day of the ceremony.

Sample Wedding Ceremony

(Processional)

Introduction

Dearly beloved, we are gathered here in the presence of God and this company to unite this man and this woman in holy matrimony. This ceremony is intended to seal God's blessings upon this union and serve as a testimony to all that marriage is, by God's design, both sacred and honorable.

(The Congregation may be Seated)

Charge to the Congregation

The Bible teaches that marriage is to be a permanent relationship of one man and one woman committed for life. Our Lord God declares in His Word "that a man shall leave his father and mother and unite with his wife in the building of a home, and the two shall become one flesh." To ignore God is to be ignorant of life's most precious truth.

Who gives this bride to be married?

Special Music   (Special Music can be included as desired)

Charge to Bride and Groom

Bride and Groom, marriage is an intimate companionship which involves both mutual commitment and equal responsibility. When you share in the joys of your life together, your happiness will be doubled; and when you share the sorrows, your sadness will be diminished to half. Through good and bad, God will make a way for you both.

You are charged by this pastor before these witnesses to dedicate your home to God the Creator. You are expected to take His Word, the Bible, as your guide and give faithful attendance to His body the Church. You can expect that when these two mighty institutions, marriage and Christ's Church, the combined strength will reward you with both temporal and eternal happiness.

Consecration Prayer

Let us pray: Lord of life and love, we humbly submit this couple into Your most Holy presence as candidates for your blessings in marriage and home. As Your divine providence has brought them together, may it now lead them to give themselves first to You and then to each other. Give them strength and patience to live their lives in a manner that will mutually bless themselves and honor Your Holy Name. We ask this in the name of Your Son Jesus Christ. Amen

(The couple will join hands and recite the following vows)

Vows

Groom do you take Bride to be your wife; will you commit yourself to her happiness and welfare, and to her usefulness in God's kingdom; and will you promise to love, honor, and trust her in sickness and in health, in adversity and prosperity, so long as you both shall live? *(I do)*

Bride do you take Groom to be your husband; will you commit yourself to his happiness and welfare, and to his usefulness in God's kingdom; and will you promise to love, honor, trust him in sickness and in health, in adversity and prosperity, so long as you both shall live? *(I do)*

(Pass bouquet and exchange rings)

Minister's Charge to Bride and Groom

Groom and Bride will you please face each other and as a token of your vows, you will now give and receive the rings.

Ring Exchange

Groom, please place the ring on Bride's finger and repeat after me: *'Bride, with this ring/ I pledge my life and love to you/ in the name of the Father/ and the Son/ and the Holy Spirit.'*

Bride, please place the ring on Groom's finger and repeat after me: *'Groom, with this ring/ I pledge my life and*

8

love to you/ in the name of the Father/ and the Son/ and the Holy Spirit.'

Minister's Blessing

Since this couple has made these commitments before God and this assembly, by the authority of God and according to the laws of the state of California, I declare that Bride and Groom are now husband and wife.

Groom and Bride, please face me. You are no longer two independent persons but one. Your lives will change dramatically from this day forward. Though Satan may tempt you to forsake these vows and even though others you meet along life's way might not encourage the sanctity of your union, always remember that Scripture warns; "What God has joined together, let no man separate."

Unity Candle
(Optional)

As the Bride and Groom have now joined together as one I will them and the congregation to hear the Lord's Prayer:

Our Father who art in haven, Hallowed be Thy name. Thy kingdom come. Thy will be done in earth, as it is in heaven. Give us this day our daily bread.

And forgive us our debts, as we forgive our debtors. And lead us not into temptation, but deliver us from evil: For Thine is the kingdom, and the power, and the glory, forever. Amen.

Conclusion

Groom, you may kiss the bride.

Groom and Bride please stand and face the congregation. It is now my distinct privilege to introduce to you Mr. & Mrs. Groom and Bride Groombride.

(Please stand for the benediction):

The grace of our Lord Jesus Christ and the love of God and the fellowship of His Holy Spirit be with you all. Amen (Recessional)

(When Children are involved, the following addition might be used)

Children

Bride and Groom, you bring ?? child(ren) and two families into this very special bond of matrimony. Do you promise to love these children and support them in their growth as your own and as God's entrustment to you?

Premarital Counseling Guide

Initial Consultation

If the couple has already set a wedding date, this meeting should take place approximately five months before the wedding day. It isn't necessary for the couple to prepare ahead of time for this first meeting. The minister will need to be prepared and have a mental outline of what to accomplish. That outline should include the following.

A. Get to know the couple and to make them feel comfortable and at ease with you, your spouse, and with the counseling process.

B. Discern the spiritual condition of the counselees, and the degree to which each is familiar with the spiritual history and commitment of the other.

C. Discern problem areas which might disqualify the couple for marriage, and determine if the couple meets the qualifications for marriage.

D. Come to an understanding of the necessity of sexual purity prior to their marriage.

E. Outline the counseling process and what will be required of the couple.

Schedule at least one other meeting, about a month later, and outline what will be covered then.

F. Clarify that no announcements should be sent out until approval by the counseling couple is given and communicated to the minister and church Office.

G. Tell the couple that this final approval will not be given until after the third meeting.

Counseling Guidelines

The following questions will be helpful to ask (Keeping notes is a good idea as well for the couple's file and later personal review):

A. How did the two of you meet?

B. How long have you known each other?

C. How long have you been dating?

D. Are you formally engaged?

E. How and why did you decide that you should get married?

F. When do you plan to get married? Where? By whom?

G. Why do you want to get married?

H. Is it your desire to have a Christian ceremony and Christian wedding?

I. To the best of your knowledge, what is a Christian marriage?

J. How is a Christian service and marriage different from other marriages?

L. How do your friends and family (including children) feel about your engagement?

M. Have any of them expressed concerns? If so, what are they?

O. Have either of you been married before? (More questions should follow if yes)

P. Have either of you been "in love" before? How many times? How long ago was the last time? What is there about your present relationship that makes it different from those past instances which did not last?

Q. Describe the spiritual dimension of your relationship up to this time? How do you want your spiritual relationship to improve?

R. Describe both the strengths and the weaknesses of your mate. What is it about your mate that attracted you? What potential problems do you anticipate in your marriage?

S. Have you been involved in pornography in the past or are you at present?

Although there is a lot to do in this first meeting, there are four things that must take priority.

First, and most important is this question: Do both the bride and groom profess faith in the Lord? The church cannot be expected to be involved in the wedding if this question is not answered affirmatively. Other arrangements can be made and the minister may use discretion here, but the binding of a believer with an unbeliever is always a risky proposition.

A. Does the couple talk about their faith with each other?

B. Are they confident about the other's conversion, and is it true faith so far as they can tell?

C. Does the couple seem to have an interest in spiritual things?

D. How well do they really know each other?

E. How well do they communicate about spiritual things?

As you might guess, this approach can open up some wonderful and meaningful discussion. It's great to hear a couple talk about the Lord, what He has done in their life, and how He is still at work. This approach can also completely stump the couple! Should that be the case, rather than allow them to "wing it," make this an assignment they will be ready to do at the next meeting.

The church's Pre-Marriage Counseling and/or Wedding Process, states that after the first meeting you and the Wedding Officiant are to decide if the couple qualifies to continue. Since you are postponing this requirement to the next meeting, this won't be completed. Don't worry about it. Pre-Marriage counseling is a process, and it's better to get to the heart of the matter rather than to complete a checklist.

Second, is the couple committed to a Christian marriage as defined in the Scripture? Is there an understanding of mutual respect and consideration based on the biblical notion of Ephesians 5:21-33: *"Submit to one another out of reverence for Christ. 22 Wives, submit yourselves to your own husbands as you do to the Lord. 23 For the husband is the head of the wife as Christ is the head of the church, his body, of which he is the Savior. 24 Now as the church submits to Christ, so also wives should submit to their husbands in everything. 25 Husbands, love your wives, just as Christ loved the church and gave himself up for her 26 to make her holy, cleansing her by the washing with water through the word, 27 and to present her to himself as a radiant church, without stain or wrinkle or any other blemish, but holy and blameless. 28 In this same way, husbands ought to love their wives as their own bodies. He who loves his wife loves himself. 29 After all, no one ever hated their own body, but they feed and care for their body, just as Christ does the church— 30 for we are members of his body. 31 "For this reason a man will leave his father and mother and be united to his wife, and the two will become one flesh." 32 This is a profound mystery—but I am talking about Christ and the church. 33 However, each one of you also must love his wife as he loves himself, and the wife must respect her husband."* (NIV)

If the couple is not committed in this way, it will be impossible for them to reconcile their relationship with God's plan for couples. A Christian marriage is a lifelong building project that begins on the foundation of God's Word. The couple must express a desire to be in God's Word on a regular basis and to worship and fellowship with other believers.

Third, does the couple have parental approval? Although not necessarily a biblical requirement for marriage, it can be inferred and is very important. Lack of parental approval is a huge red flag! Granting approval without parental consent should be an extreme exception. The church desires and expects parental approval. If you find yourself in a situation where you don't have parental approval, proceed with much prayer and caution. Take some time and find out the reason.

If possible, meet with the parents and have them articulate their concern. You may want to devote an entire meeting or more just to address this issue. Consult with other Pre-Marriage Counselors who may have experienced this situation, and certainly seek the counsel of the Elders and Deacons of the church.

Fourth, and somewhat uncomfortable to discuss, is sexual purity. To be specific, you need to find out if the couple is involved physically and to what extent. If they are involved physically, communicate clearly the expectation that from here on to the wedding, they must commit to refraining from physical intimacy. Tell the couple you will check with them at each meeting on how they are doing on their commitment. You also need to find out if they have been involved physically with others, and have they discussed it? Although potentially very hurtful, it is better for the couple to address this issue now rather that after they are married. You might ask, *"How do you bring up the subject of sexual purity tactfully?"* The best way to start is to look at God's Word on the subject. Have the couple turn to and read Ephesians 5:3, I Thessalonians 4:1-8 and Hebrews 13:4. Then ask them where they stand in relation to these verses. Let the discussion proceed from there.

Another difficult discussion to have, but necessary, is the issue of pornography and/or sexual abuse. Many in our body have witnessed firsthand the tragic result of pornography and sexual abuse on individuals and married couples. You might have to meet privately, men with men, women with women, in order for this to surface as an issue to address.

A Word About Divorce

Many, if not most people, both within and outside the church have had marital problems that led to separation or divorce. Causal factors include infidelity, spousal abuse, alcohol or chemical dependency and various other issues similar issues.

The matter is one where many of have had differences of opinion on whether or not the Bible allows for divorce and/or remarriage. Seeking then, to work from a thoroughly Biblical approach on the issue, it the intention of this chapter to clarify the matter. First, marriage is an exalted union between a man and a woman, instituted by God in creation with His intention that couples honor their commitment to each other for life. Christian fellowship is to be a place where the highest level of commitment to marriage is recognized and resources are provided to build and strengthen those marriages. However, if a marriage fails then Christian fellowship demands a place be set aside where God's grace can work to institute a process of healing and restoration in accordance with Biblical principles.

What follows is a general overview and summary of Scripture's teaching on the subject:

- God instituted marriage. His revealed will is that couples honor their vows (Gen.2:18-24; Matt.19:4-6).
- God introduced legislation on divorce in the Old Testament (Deut.24:1-4) to help control a situation which had become chaotic, which was grossly unfair to women, and which led to untold suffering for women and children. The law permitted divorce for

serious offense, made divorce formal and serious, and permitted remarriage.

- In a society where men continued to divorce their wives for ridiculous reasons, Jesus stressed the sanctity and permanence of marriage as God's plan from the beginning (Matt.19:3-9). Jesus permitted divorce for "marital unfaithfulness" (*porneia = every kind of unlawful sexual intercourse,* including incest, homosexuality, adultery).

- Divorce on this ground of *"marital unfaithfulness"* permitted remarriage to take place (this concession was recognized by rival rabbinical schools; that Jesus allowed remarriage is also clear from His statement that remarriage for any other reason constitutes adultery. Adultery is only possible if one remarries). Marriage after divorce for any other reason was designated by Jesus as adultery.

- Those divorced before becoming Christians, whatever the reason(s), are forgiven in Christ and may now marry as Christians for the first time (2 Cor.5:17).

- In the case of a Christian married to a non-Christian, God's desire is that they stay together (1 Cor.7:12-16). However, if the non-Christian leaves because of the faith of the believer, the Christian may divorce (the meaning of "no longer bound") and remarry (7:39).

- In Ephesians 5:21-33 the covenant bond of marriage is described in the context of mutual submission, with the love of Christ for the church as the model of the love a husband and wife have for each other.

At Calvary we acknowledge Scripture as the authoritative Word of God and our guide for faith and practice. Therefore, we will diligently seek to be guided by Scripture as we uphold the biblical standards of marriage. Our intent here is not to try and cover every conceivable

18

situation that might arise, rather to give insight into the position of Calvary as we seek to understand and apply Scriptural teaching. As a general rule we will operate within these guidelines:

1. God instituted marriage as a lifetime relationship between a man and a woman. The biblical understanding of marriage will at all times be the primary focus of our teaching and we will provide a variety of resources for marriage enrichment and growth that will help couples maintain the strength of their marriages.

2. In those cases where divorce is being contemplated our first efforts will always be directed toward reconciliation and healing of the marriage. Even in cases where biblical grounds exist for the divorce, the first effort will be toward reconciliation and healing.

3. When divorce occurs and the divorce is for reasons other than what the Bible allows, and should that person remarry, *"adultery"* will have been committed. The sin of adultery, like all sin, requires repentance.

4. Where people, though divorced/remarried for reasons other than what Scripture allows, sincerely acknowledge and confess their sins, we acknowledge that this sin, like all sin, is fully forgiven by God (1 John 1:9). Therefore, as a church we must extend the same level of forgiveness, and this person will receive full, unqualified acceptance by the church. This person has not committed the unpardonable sin and our understanding of God's forgiveness would permit membership and service (assuming the normal standards of spiritual maturity and qualifications are evident), even as a member of the pastoral staff.

5. There may be times in a marriage involving two believers, when serious issues like physical and/or sexual abuse would seem to necessitate a separation or divorce. Every effort should be made to seek healing and reconciliation. If this is not possible, we do not believe that God is telling an innocent victim of abuse, *"You must remain single the rest of your life."* What would be the purpose of such a position? If God gave divorce laws to protect people, where is the grace? We are not saying that God approves of divorce, but are saying that He sometimes disapproves of its alternatives more than He disapproves of divorce and remarriage. The covenant bond described in Eph.5:21-33 has been broken.

6. In cases where divorce/remarriage is entered into casually when biblical grounds do not exist—and where the individuals involved neither recognize the teaching of Scripture or the seriousness of the sin involved—the Pastor and Lay Ministers will be asked to consider appropriate action that could lead to measures of discipline.

7. Some of the situations involving divorce and/or remarriage can be very complex. At Calvary we ask our pastoral staff as they minister to couples who come to them, to make decisions regarding remarriage in the context of the guidelines stated in this document.

8. There are times, with permission of the people involved, that the request for marriage is discussed with other members of the pastoral staff in order to receive their suggestions and counsel.

9. At all times every effort is made to act in faithful accord with the teachings of Scripture and in the

spirit of forgiving grace extended to each of us in Jesus Christ.

Renewal of Wedding Vows

Invocation Prayer: **Minister**

Dear Lord, You tell us in Scripture that wherever two or more are gathered in Your name, there You will be also. We humbly request Your presence here with us now. Please be with us, bless us, and bless the sacred union of *Man's Name* and *Woman's Name*. Amen.

Introduction:

Dearly beloved, we are gathered here today to reaffirm the vows of *Man's Name* and *Woman's Name*, who for the past ?? years have held to the promise of Biblical matrimony. Marriage is a most honorable estate created by God to reflect the union of Christ and His Church. As Christ loved the Church and gave Himself up for Her; may *Man's Name* and *Woman's Name* love and respect each other till death do them part. When Christ performed His miracle at the wedding party in Cana, turning water into wine, He demonstrated His respect for both marriage and happiness. The Bible commends marriage to be honored as a sacred union in the eyes of God and the laws of the State.

Man's Name and *Woman's Name*, the Apostle Paul in his first letter to the Corinthians, chapter 13 describes love as:

"Patient and kind; Not jealous or proud; Love is not rude, selfish or irritable; Love doesn't keep a record of wrongs, but rejoices in what's right; Love never gives up…Meanwhile these three remain: faith, hope, and love; but the greatest of these is love."

While God gives life to us individually, the first real lesson in living is that of learning to get along with others, especially those in our immediate family. Simply put; we learn to love by being loved. Learning to love and learning to live peacefully among others is one of life's greatest challenges and one in which you've thrived as a couple for these many years.

As your experience has no-doubt found, loving God first enables a couple to love each other more genuinely. To love God first and foremost means loving one's spouse more completely and more satisfactorily. The measure of true love is demonstrated in the person of Christ who freely loved us and gave Himself as a sacrifice for us. Just as His love for us is given freely and unconditionally, may you grow in your love for each other as His faithful disciples.

Charge   Minister

Man's Name and *Woman's Name*, I charge you here today before these witnesses attest to the following vows:

Woman's Name will you continue to have *Man's Name* as your husband; do you reaffirm your love for him; and will you keep him, and honor him in sickness and in health; and forsaking all others, be faithful to him as long as you both shall live? I do

Man's Name will you continue to have *Woman's Name* as your wife; do you reaffirm your love for her, and will you keep her, and honor her in sickness and in health; and forsaking all others, be faithful to her as long as you both shall live? I do

Prayer of blessing   Minister

Man's Name, please place the ring on *Woman's Name's* finger and repeat after me: "*Woman's Name*, I pledge my life and love to you/ To respect and honor you/ Till death do us part/ And with this ring I renew my vow. Amen"

Woman's Name, please place the ring on *Man's Name's* finger and repeat after me:

Man's Name, I pledge my life and love to you/ To respect and honor you/ Till death do us part/ And with this ring I renew my vow. Amen

Man's Name and *Woman's Name* as you have now reaffirmed these vows first made ?? years ago;

I charge that you faithfully commit yourselves to one another as unique individuals and as one in holy matrimony. Amen.

Since *Man's Name* and *Woman's Name* have renewed their vows and pledged their love and faithfulness to each other, it is my pleasure to re-affirm that they are man and wife.

Man's Name, you may kiss your bride.

I am pleased to introduce to you the *Names*.

Man's Name and *Woman's Name* keep in mind the words of our Lord Jesus Christ in Matthew 19 where He tells us that; "A man will leave his father and mother and be united to his wife, and the two will become one flesh. So they are no longer two, but one. Therefore, what God has joined together, let man not separate."

Funerals and the Bible

The Bible provides minimal information regarding funeral and burials. Corpses were generally buried in the ground, Gen. 23:4,6, 8, only Joseph is said to have been embalmed and put in a coffin, Gen. 50:26. Mourners at funerals included family members Gen. 37:34,  acquaintances 1 Sam. 15:35 and, at times, professional mourners Eccl. 12:5. Mourning included weeping Gen. 23:2, wearing sackcloth Is. 15:3, cutting one's hair Jer. 7:29, fasting 2 Sam. 1:11, and throwing ashes on oneself Ezek. 27:30. A procession of mourners was expected to carry the corpse to the burial site 2 Sam. 3:31-34.

Standard Memorial Service

Invocation Prayer

Scripture Reading: **Psalm 23**

The LORD is my shepherd; I shall not want.

He makes me to lie down in green pastures; he leads me beside the still waters.

Yea, though I walk through the valley of the shadow of death, I will fear no evil; for

You are with me; your rod and Your staff, they comfort me.

You prepare a table before me in the presence of my enemies; you anoint my head with oil; my cup runs over.

Surely goodness and mercy shall follow me all the days of my life; and I will dwell in the house of the LORD forever. (NKJV)

Funeral Message
"God's Love"

1 Jn 4:15-16 reads, "If anyone acknowledges that Jesus is the Son of God, God lives in him and he in God. And so we know and rely on the love God has for us. God is love. Whoever lives in love lives in God, and God in him." When someone we know and love dies some of the toughest questions in life arise in our minds. "What has happened to them?" "Where are they now?" "Will I ever see them again?" Questions that express our deepest longings, but are unanswerable without some semblance of faith. It is in times like these that God gives us the faith needed to carry on, and the hope necessary to start again. But more important than faith or hope is love. Not just any love. But God's love.

The Apostle Paul writes in 1 Cor 13:13, "And now these three remain: faith, hope and love. But the greatest of these is love." Faith can set our hearts in the right direction when times are tough. Hope can raise our spirits when the pressures of this world bear down on us hard. But only God's love can see us through to life's ultimate end and guarantee that He will never leave us or forsake us.

1 Jn 4:15-16 says, "If anyone acknowledges that Jesus is the Son of God, God lives in him and he in God. And so we know and rely on the love God has for us. God is love. Whoever lives in love lives in God, and God in him."

Obituary (An obituary from the local paper is adequate)

Scripture Reading   Psalm 39

"Show me, O LORD, my life's end and the number of my days; let me know how fleeting is my life. You have made my days a mere handbreadth; the span of my years is as nothing before you. Each man's life is but a breath. But now, Lord, what do I look for? My hope is in you... " (NIV)

Prayer of Committal (Extemporaneous)

Benediction   **Jude 1:24-25**

"Now unto him that is able to keep you from falling, and to present you faultless before the presence of his glory with exceeding joy, To the only wise God our Savior, be glory and majesty, dominion and power, both now and ever. Amen." (KJV)

Standard Graveside Service

Invocation Prayer

Scripture Reading   **Revelation 1:17-18**

"...Do not be afraid. I am the First and the Last. I am the Living One; I was dead, and behold I am alive for ever and ever!"

Scripture Reading   **John 14:19**

"...Because I live, you also will live."

Scripture Reading   **Revelation 14:13**

"...Blessed are the dead who die in the Lord from now on." "Yes," says the Spirit, "they will rest from their labor, for their deeds will follow them."

Obituary (An obituary from the local paper is adequate)

A newspaper obituary is appropriate or something from the family. Include the deceased person's date of birth and death as well as places of birth and death. Include any military service or awards.

Family Remembrances (Invite family members to speak)

Prayer of Committal   (Extemporaneous)

Scripture Reading   **1 Cor. 15:51-58**   **Minister**

"Listen, I tell you a mystery: We will not all sleep, but we will all be changed--in a flash, in the twinkling of an eye, at the last trumpet. For the trumpet will sound, the dead will be raised imperishable, and we will be changed. For the perishable must clothe itself with the imperishable, and the mortal with immortality. When the perishable has been clothed with the imperishable, and the mortal with immortality, then the saying that is written will come true: "Death has been swallowed up in victory."

"Where, O death, is your victory? Where, O death, is your sting?" The sting of death is sin, and the power of sin is the law. But thanks be to God! He gives us the victory through our Lord Jesus Christ. Therefore, my dear brothers, stand firm. Let nothing move you. Always give yourselves fully to the work of the Lord, because you know that your labor in the Lord is not in vain."

Benediction Prayer (Extemporaneous)

A Note About Extemporaneous Prayers

Extemporaneous prayer simply means a prayer that is offered without notes or prompted assistance. This is simply a prayer from the minister's heart to God's ear intended to communicate worship to God as well as a verbal testimony to all listeners. There's no need for flowery speech or the use of vague religious terms, just a simple acknowledge to God in whose trust the service stands. Brief is best.

Standard Military Funeral Message

In Scripture, God is often referred to as the *"Lord of Hosts."* The Hb word *"hosts"* means *"armies."* In this sense, God is the Commander of the heavenly army. Jesus, as our Commander in the flesh, had an encounter with a Roman soldier who asked Him to heal a servant. Jesus would later say of this Centurion, that He hadn't seen such faith in all of Israel. As one who has served in the military myself, I like to think that soldiers are uniquely suited to trusting their chain-of-command. While *"foxhole faith"* tends to fade with time, a lasting trust in God prevails throughout the years and follows us into our transition from death to eternal life.

God offers us the confident assurance that when our earthly existence is over, we will leave the tents of our earthly lives and dwell forever in His permanent home. This may be the only life we've known, but there's another life coming we're told in 1 Corinthians 15:51. Paul says, *"Listen, I tell you a mystery: We will not merely sleep, but we'll all be changed—in a flash, in the twinkling of an eye, at the last trumpet. For the trumpet will sound and the dead will be raised imperishable, and we'll be changed. For the perishable must put on the imperishable, and the mortal immortality... then the saying will come true: 'Death has been swallowed up in victory.'*

...The sting of death is sin, and the power of sin is the law. But thanks be to God! He gives us the victory through our Lord Jesus Christ. (NIV)

May God's promises be the measure of our hope and expectations.

Prayer: *God Almighty, we close this brief service with hope in Your promise and faith in Your ability to transform us. We are not overwhelmed by loss or drowning in hopelessness. Nonetheless, we seek Your strength in the coming days as we struggle to deal with what has happened, and we know You will walk with us. We trust You even though we don't understand fully Your timing or purpose. We know You love us and we thank You for the gift of life and the promise of life eternal through Your Son, our Savior, the Lord Jesus, in Whose Name we pray, Amen.*

Standard Memorial Message
(A Memorial Service is a service without the deceased's body.)

Introduction

Frequently pastors and churches are called upon to perform the undesirable task of memorial services like this one. Unlike weddings, dedications, and baptisms, the ceremony is an unwelcome reminder that life must include sadness and tragedy as well as joy and triumph. It's a time when our deepest beliefs and hopes are challenged and our daily worries are revealed to be petty concerns at best. This world is an odd mix of believers and unbelievers forced to suffer the ultimate disbelief and doubt that we call death. Whatever beliefs you've brought with you here this day; my prayer is that the beliefs of simple Christians like myself will serve to provide some small piece of hope.

Consolation

No matter how deep the despair or how painful the loss, whatever hope we have as disciples comes from our faith and trust in Jesus Christ. Through the shifting centuries full of promising expectations followed by the discouraging realities of endless disappointments, for 2,000 years our hope has remained the same. Men die, but Jesus Christ lives and we further believe that because Jesus Christ died for our sins, His resurrection can be ours as well if we trust Him as Savior and Lord. The Bible says in John 3:16 that… "God so loved the world that He gave his one and only Son, [so] that whoever believes in him shall not perish but have eternal life…" You've probably heard that verse before or maybe memorized in Sunday School, but the very next verse in that passage says this: "God did not send his Son into the world to condemn the world, but to save the world through Him. Whoever believes in [Jesus] is not condemned, but whoever does not believe [in Him] stands condemned already because he has not believed in the name of God's one and only Son."

Our existence on earth is a mere flash of life hardly noticeable in the infinity of time. But the resurrection of

Jesus Christ stands as God's unique promise in Scripture that death is not man's end.

To mourn the death of a loved one without hope is to deny that faith is stronger than life's mysteries and doubts. Yet, to rejoice in the absence of a loved one is to deny our God-given emotions of grief from loss. And so, we can only hope to find satisfactory seeds of faith in the words of our Savior who promised us that those who hunger and thirst after righteousness shall indeed be satisfied.

Conclusion

I want to close by reading the words of Jesus in John 8:12:

"I am the light of the world. Whoever follows me will never walk in darkness, but will have the light of life." (NIV) So many of us spend our lives searching in quiet desperation for some meaningful knowledge beyond what little we can actually come to understand in this life. Just when we think we've fooled ourselves and everyone around us with a rather convincing display of self-assurance and inward courage, life sends a bomb of overwhelming catastrophe and we're left with little more than a broken heart and a numbed mind. But there is hope and that is what God's Word and God's people are all about. Christian's aren't a particularly pious or good people in the religious sense, as a matter of fact we can be downright despicable, but we do know a Savior who is everything and more than anyone could ever hope to experience in this life. You see, the Christian faith is founded upon the unalterable conviction that Jesus is the only begotten Son of God. He wasn't merely a wonderful religious prophet, or just a great healer and teacher, we believe that He was and is "Immanuel," God with us. He was and is the only sacrifice worthy of erasing humankind's sin in the eyes of Almighty

God for the sake of perfect justice. We have always been convinced that Jesus is the resurrected Lord of all creatures who has promised those who believe in Him eternal life. Not just life that goes on forever as it is, but abundant life both here and hereafter.

According to John 8:12, *"Jesus is the Light."* He's a guiding light in a world that can sometimes become so dark it requires eyes of faith to see beyond the tears and sorrow. We struggle and we strive to bolster our faith with deeds worthy of God's approval. But our final rest doesn't come as a payment for our hard work or diligent service. It comes as the exclusive result of Christ's sacrifice and God's generous grace to forgive.

Baptism and Communion

Introduction

There are two symbolic ceremonies (some churches call them *"sacraments"*) in the Baptist church. They are known as *"ordinances"* and they represent two essential practices within each congregation. Those ordinances are: (1) **Baptism** and (2) **Communion** (The Lord's Supper). Along with worship style, theological tradition and various doctrines, these two elements of congregational practice are what distinguish Baptists from various other Christian denominations. Our practice of "believer's baptism" (adult only baptism) by immersion is exclusively available to those who've made a public profession of faith in Jesus Christ as Lord.

Unlike many Reform churches that teach baptism as a covenant beginning at birth, which promises God's grace upon confirmation at reaching the age of accountability, Baptists believe baptism to be a purely symbolic observance outwardly representing an inward faith. Similarly, Baptist communion services are symbolic memorial meals observed in keeping with Jesus' command to "do this in remembrance of Me." Baptists believe the supper to be symbolic and yet sacred as an act of obedience through faith in Christ. Unlike some churches that teach the elements of bread and wine actually become the body and blood of Christ, Baptists believe the elements to be symbolic, representing the substance of our faith in Christ. Baptist do not customarily use fermented wine.

The Baptist Faith and Message

The *Baptist Faith and Message* states in section 7 under the title, *Baptism and the Lord's Supper*:

> *"Christian baptism is the immersion of a believer in water in the name of the Father, the Son, and the Holy Spirit. It is an act of obedience symbolizing the believer's faith in a crucified, buried, and risen Savior, the believer's death to sin, the burial of the old life, and the resurrection to walk in newness of life in Christ Jesus. It is a testimony to his faith in the final resurrection of the dead. Being a church ordinance, it is prerequisite to the privileges of church membership and to the Lord's Supper.*
>
> *"The Lord's Supper is a symbolic act of obedience whereby members of the church, through partaking of the bread and the fruit of the vine, memorialize the death of the Redeemer and anticipate His second coming."* Matthew 3:13-17; 26:26-30; 28:19-20; Mark 1:9-11; 14:22-26; Luke 3:21-22; 22:19-20; John 3:23; Acts 2:41-42; 8:35-39; 16:30-33; 20:7; Romans 6:3-5; 1 Corinthians 10:16,21; 11:23-29; Colossians 2:12.

It should be noted that there have been no changes or revisions to these words in the BF&M since its original adoption by the Southern Baptists in 1925.

A Brief Word About Infant Baptism

One of the best resources for learning as well as understanding the issues surrounding infant and believer's baptism is the book *Baptism: Three Views,* edited by David F. Wright.

In terms of mode, the New Testament baptismal accounts actually don't require immersion since pouring may have occurred in some instances such as in Matthew

3:16 or Acts 8:38. Early church records attest to the commonly accepted fact of infant baptism, along with the third century Apostolic Tradition which refers to baptizing children who were *"not yet able to speak."*

As with Abraham's circumcision, baptism can be viewed as a sign and seal of the righteousness that comes by grace through faith. But where believers' baptism emphasizes what the believer does in responding by faith, the baptism of an infant (paedobaptism) emphasizes what Christ alone has done.

Various *"household"* baptism texts demonstrate that the Old Testament's covenant understanding of the family apparently continues into the New Testament context. It would appear that God would not promote the family unit in the Old Testament only to displace it in the new, and nothing in the New Testament suggests the family has been displaced as an integral port into God's kingdom.

"Baptism functions in relationship to the new covenant in Christ in a manner analogous to the function of circumcision in the Abrahamic covenant," writes Sinclair Ferguson. *"In a word, baptism has the same symbolic significance in relationship to fellowship with God as did circumcision."*

Jeremiah 32:38f includes the *"to you and your seed"* principle in his expression of the prophetic new covenant, as do all divine covenants prior to Pentecost. The fact that the way of salvation has always been the same, suggests that the ordinance of baptism which replaces circumcision, the previous sign of salvation, can also be given to infants. Christ specifically blesses not just children in Mark 10:13f but apparently babies as in Luke 18:15f.

While the infant baptism argument depends more upon theological ties and historical heritage, the believer's baptism argument is a bit more straightforward in reading the texts.

The believer's baptism (credobaptist) account is just easier to grasp on the surface and prove textually by biblical reference. This is not to say that it's right as opposed to the other arguments being wrong. It just means a person upon first inquiry, or with less time to commit to reading about the issue will find believer's baptism a little easier to digest.

It's been point out that few Baptists are willing to challenge the recent development of baptizing small children because of the enthusiasm for this relatively new practice. However, children tend to do what pleases their parents which may explain this trend more than spiritual revival. Plus, the whole issue of baptizing small children seems to only undermine the believer's baptism argument and indirectly agrees with some arguments held by those active in defending infant baptism.

In a nutshell, the Bible doesn't precisely specify whether infants can be baptized or only believing adults. The early church's apparent variety of approaches on the issue make it difficult without some background. Tony Lane says, *"The silences are there to leave the church liberty to vary its practice to suit different circumstances. They sanction the variety of practice that we see in the early church."* While Lane's view is interesting, it seems a little too personally oriented for most. He argues that churches should be allowed the freedom to decide what they want baptism to mean. However, it hard to imagine Paul not expecting uniformity among the churches when it comes to this issue.

A Brief History of Baptism
Old Testament

Although there's no explicit reference to baptism in the Old Testament, some point out that baptism was evidently practiced towards the end of Old and the beginning of the New Testament period by Jews as an initiation for Gentile converts. There are references to various practices that apparently manifested themselves in Christian baptism, such as the use of water for ceremonial purification, the pouring out of the Holy Spirit on individuals, and (possibly)...circumcision.

Whether circumcision was an Old Testament form similar to, or the same as, baptism is a theological decision. Those who favor a link between circumcision and baptism argue that, just as circumcision marked a child as being part of the old covenant of Abraham, so infant baptism marks a child as being part of the new covenant of Jesus Christ.

John Calvin, one of the founders of the Reformed Church, comments: "...*just as circumcision, which was a kind of badge to the Jews, assuring them that they were adopted as the people and family of God, was their first entrance into the Church, while they, in their turn, professed their allegiance to God, so now we are initiated by baptism, so as to be enrolled among his people, and at the same time swear unto his name.* (Calvin, *Christian Institutes*, p. 1473)

New Testament

We're introduced to Baptism in the New Testament by John the Baptist who practiced immersion of candidates in the Jordan River as evidence of their repentance. He called for a definite and deliberate *"baptism of repentance for the forgiveness of sins."* This concept of a baptism as a sign of repentance, and the forgiveness of sins later became an important element (although not, of course, the sole element) of Christian baptism.

Symbolism and Sacramentalism

By the fourth century, many people began putting off baptism until they were near death, so that they could continue to live a sinful life and get it all cleaned up before dying. When candidates were baptized in the early church, they were expected to live pure and chaste lives from that point on. So there was a temptation to hold off on Christian baptism with its demands for purity until nearing death in order to avoid a lifetime requirement of right living. So much for human reasoning!

Constantine wasn't baptized until 337 A.D, shortly before his death. It is described by Eusebius: *"Being at length convinced that his life was drawing to a close, he felt the time was come at which he should seek purification from sins of his past career, firmly believing that whatever errors he had committed as a mortal man, his soul would be purified from them through the efficacy of the mystical words and the salutary waters of baptism..."* (Eusebius, p. 809/11)

Churches like Calvary practice immersion based on the profession of the candidate's faith as administered by a congregation of like faith and practice. While we acknowledge the significance of infants and practice the dedication of infants, just as Jesus was dedicated at the temple, we do not baptize them. A person must be to the age of accountability (knowing moral right from wrong) as determined by church leaders to understand the Gospel message and respond to it individually. A baptismal candidate is then brought into the water by the minister and introduced by name then asked if they have professed faith in Jesus as Lord. So long as the candidate agrees, the minister then proceeds to immerse them once in the name of the Father, Son and Holy Spirit.

A Brief History Communion

For centuries, Roman Catholics received only bread during Communion. No one knows exactly when the practice became common—worshipers in the early church shared bread, wine, and often a whole meal—But as the sacramental elements took on greater significance in and of themselves some began to believe that they actually became flesh and blood upon consecration. Thus, greater pains were taken to preserve and protect them. Some early Christians were accused of being *"cannibals"* because they were said to be eating the literal flesh and blood of Christ. By the fourteenth and early fifteenth centuries some called for a return the common partaking of both elements but the Catholic Church was entrenched in its insistence on bread alone. This position was set by the Council of Trent, in the sixteenth century then mitigated by Vatican II in the 1960s. The documents of Vatican II allow for Communion of both kinds in certain circumstances (a person's first Communion after baptism, for example), but many churches have extended the practice much farther.

The Eastern Orthodox Church, like the Catholic church, asserts a mystical *"real presence"* of Christ in the elements, but it defines *"real presence"* a bit differently. According to the Department of Religious Education for Orthodox Church in America, *"The Orthodox Church denies the doctrine that the Body and the Blood of the eucharist are merely intellectual or psychological symbols of Christ's Body and Blood. ... On the other hand, however, the Orthodox tradition does use the term 'symbols' for the eucharistic gifts. It calls the service a 'mystery' and the sacrifice of the liturgy a 'spiritual and bloodless sacrifice.'"*

Virtually all Protestant churches serve bread and a grape juice during Communion, but the similarities end there. The bread of some communions is made of regular yeast loaf and some use unleavened bread. Among those churches that used unleavened breads, some do it primarily because of the Old Testament precedent set by God when He instructed the Israelites to prepare it before their exodus from Egypt. (see Exodus 12, Deuteronomy 16, Luke 22, etc.).

Congregants in churches may pass the bread on a plate, receive it from the front of the sanctuary, or have it served to them individually. The grape juice also may be passed in a common cup, distributed in single-serving cups.

Calvary is typical of many evangelical churches today. We practice Communion based on the Gospel texts given by Christ during the last meal with His disciples. It is explained at the beginning of the ordinance that the meal is intended for believers only. Using the Apostle Paul's admonitions against frivolousness in the meal, everyone is invited to partake in hopes that each congregant will decide rightly whether they should participate or not.

Communion Q&A

In accordance with the teaching of our Lord and the practice of likeminded Southern Baptist Churches Calvary recognizes two ordinances: Baptism and the Lord's Supper or Communion.

The Apostle Paul states in 1 Corinthians 11:23-25: *"The Lord Jesus on the night when he was betrayed took a loaf of bread, and when he had given thanks, he broke it and said, 'This is my body that is for you Do this in remembrance of me.' In the same way he took the cup also, after supper, saying, 'This cup is the new covenant in my blood. Do this, as often as you drink it, in remembrance of me.'"* And in Luke 24:30-31: *"When Jesus was at table with them, he took bread, blessed and broke it, and gave it to them. Then their eyes were opened, and they recognized him."*

What is an Ordinance?

It is a traditional practice of separate worship in which, according to Scripture, Christians are instituted by Christ to do as He instructed. In the practice of baptism and communion we invite God's Holy Spirit to make tangible the grace, forgiveness, and presence of His Son Jesus Christ.

The communion meal recalls the table fellowship Jesus shared with his disciples at the last meal recorded in the Gospels and in particular the Last Supper on the night before his death. Throughout its history these Biblical events have been central to the Church's worship life.

What is the Meaning of Communion?

An intimate experience of fellowship in which the whole church family in every time and place is present and divisions are overcome;

What elements are used and What do they mean?

The bread and juice represent the crucified and risen Christ. The bread recalls the unleavened loaf that God instructed the Israelites to prepare as He led them out of Egypt. The juice recalls Jesus statement of the New Covenant in His blood.

What words are used?

At the heart of the service are Jesus' words about the bread and the cup from the Biblical account of the Last Supper.

How is Communion served?

A variety of practices are acceptable, including the sharing of a common loaf or the use of individual wafers or cubes of bread and the sharing of a common cup or of individual cups either at the alter or in the pews. Care should be taken to ensure that the full meaning of the ordinance is communicated by the way the elements are used and served. The pastor presides, normally assisted by elders or deacons.

Who may receive Communion?

The meal is "open to all believers who wish to participate and to share in the fellowship of God's people." Some visitors may not choose to participate are to have their decision respected.

What about children?

In many Christian churches baptized children and even infants are able to receive communion. However, Calvary insists that only professing believers participate in this meal. We welcome children and families but ask that only those having been baptized receive Communion.

How often is Communion served?

In the early church Communion may have been served weekly, a practice continued and encouraged by some Protestants as well as Catholics. Gradually the frequency of communion was decreased to add to its significance and to avoid mundane attitudes toward it. Calvary observes the Lord's Supper on the first Sunday of every month as well as on Christmas Eve and Good Friday.

Summary

Baptism and Communion comprise the worship ordinances of a Baptist church. In keeping with the traditions of Scripture we recognize the essential and sacred importance of these services and yet acknowledge the purely symbolic meaning of both practices. Although we don't necessarily share the same viewpoints as others in these areas of faith, we do agree in general that what Christ has instituted all disciples should follow in observance faithfully. While it's never intended to be an insult that we hold these ordinances as symbols and not sacraments, we genuinely believe that their value to believers is found in faith not function.

Sample Baptismal Service

In the Baptist tradition, baptismal services are usually integrated into an existing order of worship at the beginning or at the end. Below is an idea of how most are done:

Minister: Welcomes those in attendance drawing special attention to those family members and friends in attendance for this specific baptism.

Introduction: In accordance with Scripture I present to this congregation *Candidate's Name* for baptism.

Scripture Reading: **Matthew 3:13-17**

In Matthew's Gospel, we're told in 3:13ff that "Jesus came from Galilee to the Jordan River to be baptized by John the Baptist. [14] But John tried to deter him, saying, "I need to be baptized by You, and do You come to me?"

[15] Jesus replied, "Let it be so now; it is proper for us to do this to fulfill all righteousness." Then John consented.

[16] As soon as Jesus was baptized, He went up out of the water. At that moment heaven was opened, and He saw the Spirit of God descending like a dove and alighting on Him. [17] And a voice from heaven said, "This is My Son, whom I love; with Him I am well pleased."

Explanation

The occasion of Jesus' public baptism was recorded for all future generations to see the perfect embodiment of the triune God revealed in glory from heaven. The testimony directly from heaven of the Father's pleasure with the Son and the descending of the Holy Spirit upon Jesus is a picture of the trinitarian nature of God. It also depicts the work of the Father, Son, and Spirit in the salvation of those

Jesus came to save. The Father loves the elect from before the foundation of the world (Ephesians 1:4); He sends His Son to seek and save the lost (Luke 19:10); and the Spirit convicts of sin (John 16:8) and draws the believer to the Father through the Son. All the glorious truth of the mercy of God through Jesus Christ is on display at His baptism.

Sample Communion Service #1

When Jesus gathered His disciples into the upper room for their last supper together, it was on the occasion of the Jewish Passover and within hours of His betrayal by Judas. While their Jewish tradition expected them to observe the ceremony that looked back at the deliverance of their Israelite ancestors from Egypt. The situation at hand brought a much deeper meaning to what going on that night. Though no longer slaves to Pharaoh, Israel herself had come under the plague of sin. And while Moses was long dead and buried, the Messiah he had hoped for was in the room that night.

Our Savior set aside the *"Lord's Supper,"* as a time of worship when His church would come together and celebrate our most sacred faith. That Jesus was sent by God to save us from Adam's curse and deliver us by His grace to eternal life through His sacrifice on the cross at Calvary.

That evening, the unleavened bread that traditionally represented God's provision for His people during the Exodus, Jesus here proclaims to be His body. And the fruit of the vine that had previously represented the blood of innocent lambs painted upon the doorposts to signal the death angel to pass by, Jesus says is His blood. Then, Jesus took the bread, blessed it and gave it to His disciples. Then He took the cup and instructed them to *"drink from it."*

As the body of Christ, we must always be careful not to allow this ordinance to become a legalistic ritual or a self-righteous routine. But always remember that Communion is a witness of our faith and our trust in the resurrected Savior, Jesus Christ!

Let us Pray: *"Gracious God and Loving Savior. Who's Holy Spirit lives in our hearts and surrounds us here in this*

44

house of prayer. In obedience to Your command to "break the bread and drink the cup...in remembrance of You," we now partake of Your Lord's Supper. By observing this ordinance, we covenant to repent of our sins and seriously surrender our lives to You in response to what You've have done to secure our salvation.

We acknowledge that this meal is intended for those who have professed their faith in You by Baptism and whom You have delivered from sin by your gift of grace. We quietly reflect upon the Scriptures that have told us of Your promise of a home with You in heaven.

So, we gather around the church's table of faith to worship You in the name of the Father, Son and Holy Spirit. Amen"

Scripture says that, *"...while they were eating, Jesus took bread, gave thanks and broke it, and gave it to the disciples, saying, 'Take and eat; this is my body.'"*

(Bread)

Scripture goes on to say that, *"...Jesus then took the cup, gave thanks and offered it to them, saying, 'Drink from it, all of you. This is my blood of the covenant, which is poured out for many for the forgiveness of sins. I tell you, I will not drink of this fruit of the vine from now on until that day when I drink it anew with you in my Father's kingdom.'"* (Juice)

Sample Communion Service #2

The Lord's Supper

In the OT, the Passover was the most sacred feast of the Jewish religious year. It commemorated the final plague on Egypt when the firstborn of the Egyptians died and the Israelites were spared because of the blood of a lamb that was sprinkled on their doorposts. The lamb was then roasted and eaten with unleavened bread. God's command was that throughout the generations to come the feast would be celebrated.

It was during the last supper with His disciples while observing Passover that Jesus took a loaf of bread and some wine, gave thanks and gave it to His disciples. Then, He concluded the meal by leading them out into the Mt. of Olives and it was there that Jesus was betrayed and crucified the next day.

The account of the Lord's Supper are found in all four Gospels as well as in 1 Corinthians 11 where the Apostle Paul warns that: *"whoever eats the bread or drinks the cup of the Lord in an unworthy manner will be guilty of sinning against the body and blood of the Lord. Everyone ought to examine themselves before they eat of the bread and drink from the cup. For those who eat and drink without discerning the body of Christ eat and drink judgment on themselves."*

The Apostle Paul writes in 1 Cor. 11:23ff, *"For I received from the Lord what I also passed on to you: The Lord Jesus, on the night He was betrayed, took bread, and when He had given thanks, He broke it and said, 'This is My body, which is for you; do this in remembrance of Me."* In the same way, after supper he took the cup, saying, 'This cup is the new covenant in My blood; do this, whenever you drink it, in remembrance of Me.' For whenever you eat this bread and drink this cup, you proclaim the Lord's death until He comes."

So, in obedience to the Savior we're gathered here to look back with thanksgiving for what He's done and forward in preparation for what He's yet to do.

At Calvary we pass the communion bread and cup to everyone but it's intended for those who've made a public profession of their faith in Jesus Christ by means of believer's baptism.

Prayer: *Lord God, we've received the good news that there's room at the table for repentant sinners to be seated with Your Son, our Messiah. With grateful thanks we receive Your invitation at this time.*

God, graciously prepare us to be humbled by our sins, restored by Your forgiveness, and made ready for Your final return. Stir up within us a desire to glorify of Your Son, without whom there could be no supper and no fellowship. Lord, grant this for Jesus' sake.

It was on the occasion of the Jewish Passover that Jesus called together His disciples to demonstrate what God was about to do.

Observance

Scripture says that, *"...while they were eating, Jesus took bread, gave thanks and broke it, and gave it to His disciples, saying, 'Take and eat; this is my body.'"* And so likewise we partake of this bread in communion with all saints as a symbol of obedience to Christ Jesus our Lord.

Scripture also says that, *"...Jesus then took the cup, gave thanks and offered it to them, saying, 'Drink from it, all of you. This is my blood of the covenant, which is poured out for many for the forgiveness of sins. I tell you, I will not drink of this fruit of the vine from now on until that day when I drink it anew with you in my Father's kingdom.'"* Again, we drink from this cup in symbolic commitment to our Savior who is both deserving and worthy of our worship.

Appendix B
Dedications in the Bible

A religious ceremony in which a person or a thing is set aside or consecrated to God's service. In Bible times, many different things were included in such services: The Temple 2 Chr. 2:4, a field Lev. 27:16, a house Lev. 27:14, articles of precious metal 2 Sam. 8:10, even spoils won in battle 1 Chr. 26:27. In one of the most beautiful passages in the Bible Hannah presented her young son Samuel to God in an act of child dedication 1 Sam. 1:19-28. Hannah's prayer of thanksgiving to God 1 Sam. 2:1-10 is a model of praise and dedication for all who seek to honor God through their lives.

Standard Child Dedication Service
Introduction:

This service is a commitment of parents and sponsors to offer these children and themselves in dedication to God. In this ceremony we recognize and agree that life is a gift from God and that children are God's gift to parents. The dedication of children is taught in Luke 2:22 when the infant Jesus was presented by His parents, Mary and Joseph in the Temple. (Luke 2:22-35).

Minister's Charge:

It is the privilege of this church to encourage and assist these parents and their sponsors in the proper spiritual, moral, and intellectual training of these children. It is proper that we give thanks to God for the birth of children and likewise to challenge parents to raise them in the instruction of His Word and His Will.

We pray for God's blessing upon them remembering that Jesus took the children in Matthew 19:14 and blessed them.

God instructs His people in Deuteronomy 6:4-7, to; *"Love the LORD your God with all your heart and with all your soul and with all your strength. These commandments that I give you today are to be upon your hearts. Impress them on your children. Talk about them when you sit at home and when you walk along the road, when you lie down and when you get up."* (NIV)

Covenant:

Parents, in presenting your children to the Lord, do you promise to provide them with every opportunity to learn the truths of the Christian faith; to set a Christian example for them; and to bring them up in the instruction of the Lord?

Sponsors, in accepting the responsibility to partner with these parents in the keeping of this covenant, do you promise to encourage them in the fulfillment of their promise?

Do you Church family, promise to join with these families and their sponsors in the teaching and training of these children that they may be led in due time to trust Christ as Savior and to confess Him in baptism and church membership?

If you accept this responsibility, will you indicate by standing?

Standard Anointing Service
Ministry to the Sick

Read James 5:13-15

"Is any one of you in trouble? He should pray. Is anyone happy? Let him sing songs of praise. Is any one of you sick? He should call the elders of the church to pray over him and anoint him with oil in the name of the Lord.

And the prayer offered in faith will make the sick person well; the Lord will raise him up. If he has sinned, he will be forgiven." (NIV)

Prayer

Read Mark 6:7-13

"Calling the Twelve to him, he sent them out two by two and gave them authority over evil spirits. These were his instructions: *"Take nothing for the journey except a staff—no bread, no bag, no money in your belts. Wear sandals but not an extra tunic. Whenever you enter a house, stay there until you leave that town. And if any place will not welcome you or listen to you, shake the dust off your feet when you leave, as a testimony against them."* They went out and preached that people should repent. They drove out many demons and anointed many sick people with oil and healed them." (NIV)

Anointing

Prayer

Dedication of Facility

Invocation & Prayer   Psalm 127:1   Minister

Recognition and Thanks

Presentation of Certificate/Plaque

Responsive Reading

Minister: Because we have purposed in our hearts to build facilities for the worship of our Savior Jesus Christ, I call upon this congregation to stand for the holy act of dedication. (Please Stand)

Minister: To the glory of God the Father; to the honor of Jesus Christ His Son; to the praise of the Holy Spirit...

Congregation: We dedicate this house.

Minister: Knowing there is no other name under heaven given to men by which we must be saved…

Congregation: We dedicate this house.

Minister: In obedience the command of Christ to go into all the world and preach the good news to all creation…

Congregation: We dedicate this house.

Minister: Realizing the obligation to bring up our children in the training and instruction of the Lord…

Congregation: We dedicate this house.

All: We dedicate this house to the fellowship of the saints, to the refuge of the weary, to the training of our children, to the comfort of those who mourn and to the happiness of those who share our faith.

Dedication Prayer

Licensing of Minister

The appointment given you by your fellow members this day is one that should be entered into with careful consideration. We are not sufficient of ourselves for such a responsibility But, God who has called us, "is able to make all grace abound to you, so that in all things at all time, having all that you need, you will abound in every good work."

It is imperative that you guard your conduct and speech. The measure of your godliness and zeal will be copied by others. Be concerned for the needs of the church family.

Whatever the minister's title like the first century Stephen—who was set apart for a specific ministry, you are to be full of the Spirit and wisdom, versed in the Scriptures, ready to witness and, if need be, to die for your Lord. Give careful attention as well to the office entrusted to you. As unto the Lord, fulfill all its functions. By accepting this trust, you indicate without reservation your commitment and loyalty to the message, doctrine, constitution and world-wide program of your church. Be faithful that you may enter with joy into the presence of your Lord, to whom you shall render account.

Do you now accept your office as a sacred and solemn trust from the Lord Jesus Christ, promising Him and this church to fulfill its responsibilities and ministries as indicated above to the best of your ability?
(I do)

Will you strive with God's help to be an example of Christ in the midst of those whom He has set you as leader, holding to the deep truths of the faith with a clear conscience?
(I do)

Do you, the members of this Church, acknowledge and receive this minister, entering with him into the spirit of the vows he has just made to God and this church? Do you promise to honor him, to encourage him, to cooperate with him and to pray for him, as the Word of God and the bylaws of this church admonish? The congregation will please stand as I lead us in prayer.

Appendix A
Pastoral Counseling

Informed Consent

This document has been provided to explain my services to you. At the bottom of this document you will note a signature line. After reading and discussing this document, you will be asked to sign this document. Your signature indicates that you are giving me permission to continue in our counseling relationship. Please feel free to ask any questions to clarify what you read here.

I am a Pastor at This church Baptist Church. While I have experience counseling specific issues, there are times when I feel that referring an individual to another more qualified counselor would be best. In the event that I feel that your case will be better served in the hands of another counselor I will inform you and discuss those options with you. Furthermore, at any time you may request to be referred to another counselor.

As a Pastor, I find the incorporation of spiritual insights important in many counseling situations. When I feel it is appropriate to specific situations, I will use the Bible as a counseling tool. While I do find spiritual issues important, I am also aware of the psychological sciences and I often explore what others might call "secular" understandings in my research. You will find that my counsel is a blend of Biblical understanding and secular science.

Your signature on this document states clearly that you will not discuss your relationship or your relationship difficulties outside of the counselor's office with others. In all likelihood, the advice that you will obtain from others will be biased information from sources untrained in therapeutic techniques. That information will hinder or destroy any prospect of health being brought to your relationship.

As a Pastor, I do not regularly charge for counseling services. However, if you find that these services are of significant benefit to you, you may consider an additional offering to the Benevolent Fund of the church. Your gifts would be much appreciated.

During the course of counseling, I regularly consult with individuals who are professional counselors. I have submitted myself to their oversight as a fellow counselor. When I need additional information I often consult them. When I have problems of my own, I do not hesitate to call so that I can discuss those issues. As the Pastor of the church I am also completely accountable to the church board for my actions.

Prayers for Special Occasions

The Old Testament word for prayer is t$_e$p$_e$l$_a$ meaning *"to cut"* as in cutting into one's self in order to give time to God our judge. The Psalms take up a good portion of the Old Testament and they are basically poetic prayers intended to lead God's people to worship Him for who He says He is and what He says He wants.

***

Psalms 1

1 Blessed is the one who does not walk in step with the wicked or stand in the way that sinners take or sit in the company of mockers,

2 but whose delight is in the law of the Lord, and who meditates on his law day and night.

3 That person is like a tree planted by streams of water, which yields its fruit in season and whose leaf does not wither—whatever they do prospers.

4 Not so the wicked! They are like chaff that the wind blows away.

5 Therefore the wicked will not stand in the judgment, nor sinners in the assembly of the righteous. 6 For the Lord watches over the way of the righteous, but the way of the wicked leads to destruction. (NIV)

***

Lord, I want to be blessed by You and so I will not walk in step with the wicked or stand in the way of sinners or sit in the company of mockers. Instead, Lord, I will delight Your Word and meditate on it daily.

I will expect to become a person who is like a fruitful tree planted by streams of water unlike the wicked who are like chaff that the wind blows away.

For I know Lord, that You watch over the way of the righteous, but the way of the wicked leads to destruction.

Memorial Day Prayer

Gracious Lord and God,

All glory and power belong to You. We offer this prayer in behalf of those brave ones in our military and ask You to protect and watch over them in these days of war.

Your Bible says, *"Blessed is the nation whose God is the Lord;"* make us mindful of our heritage and of who we are. You said *"Be strong and of good courage,"* this is our prayer today that as a nation we will be strong and courageous in support of our troops and their families. You said *"A king is not saved by his great army; a warrior is not delivered by his great strength;"* we humbly ask You, Oh Lord, to be our protection and strength. Defend our nation and may all of Heaven safeguard the families of our troops back home. Almighty God, when Your will so provides, please safely return our men and women home, may our nation recognized the willingness of our brave soldiers to fight for life, liberty, freedom and justice. In Jesus' name Amen.

Mother's Day Prayer

Most Gracious Heavenly Father, we thank You for our mothers to whom You have entrusted the care of every precious human life from its very beginning in the womb.

You have given to woman the capacity of participating with You in the creation of new life. Grant that every woman may come to understand the full meaning of that blessing, which gives her an unlimited capacity for selfless love for every child she may be privileged to bear, and for all Your children.

Give her courage in times of fear or pain, understanding in times of uncertainty and doubt, and hope in times of trouble.

To mothers You have given the great privilege and responsibility of being a child's first teacher and spiritual guide.

Grant that all mothers may worthily foster the faith of their children, following the example of Mary, Elizabeth, and other Christian women who followed Christ.

Help mothers to grow daily in knowledge and understanding of Your Son, Our Lord Jesus Christ, and grant them the wisdom to impart this knowledge faithfully to their children, and to all who depend upon them. Assist all those who selflessly care for the children of others -- of every age and state in life.

Grant that they may know the joy of fulfilling this motherly calling of women, whether in teaching, nursing, or in other work which recognizes and fosters the true dignity of every human being created in Your image and likeness.

May all mothers receive Your Grace abundantly in this earthly life, and may they look forward to eternal joy in Your presence in the life to come. We ask this through our Lord Jesus Christ, who lives with You and the Holy Spirit, one God, world without end. AMEN.

Thanksgiving Prayer

Gracious God, we call upon You to attend this fellowship and become our Holy Host providing the warmth of Christian friendship and the hospitality of heavenly peace. We have come together to offer our humble sacrifice of praise in thanksgiving for Your Son and our Savior Jesus Christ and for Your Holy Spirit our Comforter and

Protector. May You be blessed as You've blessed us, and may we bless those whom You've called us to minister among.

Lord, help us to remember this week;

That as we have food on our tables, there are those who are hungry;

That we have work to attend to, there are those who are jobless;

That when dwell go to our homes, that there are those who are homeless;

That when we are without pain, that there are those who are suffering.

And that by remembering these things, Lord God, may You stir within us greater compassion, diminish our complacency and raise our concern to actively help by word and deed, those who cry out for what we so often take for granted. In your name we pray. Amen.

Benediction Prayer

Now unto You our God, who is able to keep us from falling, and to present us faultless before Your presence in glory and with exceeding joy, to You our only wise God and Savior, be glory and majesty, dominion and power, both now and ever. Amen.   Jude 1:24,25

Sanctity of Human Life Prayer

Our God and Father in heaven,

We praise You as Creator and Maker of every living thing. We worship You as those whom You have redeemed by the life, death and resurrection of Your Son Jesus Christ. We thank you for this gathering of believers, and for a new year in which to serve and glorify You. We pray, that we would know the meaning of 'being in the world, but not of it' and that we'd live to please You in all things.

We pray, Lord, that Your people would see what love and justice demand of us regarding the sanctity of life, and the prevention of all things that compromise life's value from abortion to euthanasia.

To that end, give us a full measure of Your Holy Spirit to stand strong in Your Will.

That in all things, Lord, we would be faithful to Your Word, and in step with Your Holy Spirit.

In Jesus' name we pray,

Amen.

Prayer for Leaders of Government

Introduction:

The Apostle Paul tells Timothy in 1 Timothy 2:1-4, *"...to pray for all people. Ask God to help them; intercede on their behalf, and give thanks for them. Pray this way for kings and all who are in authority so that we can live peaceful and quiet lives marked by godliness and dignity. This is good and pleases God our Savior, who wants everyone to be saved and to understand the truth."*

Let us pray: "Our Lord and God. In obedience to Your command, we lift up those who lead us in government. We pray for our Mayor and City Council and all those who provide civil leadership in our local community. We pray for our State and Federal officials, that You would convict them to lead with integrity and for the welfare of this republic. While we thank You for our freedoms, we pray for those who've been elected to preserve our liberty so that we might be free to serve You in thanksgiving for the grace given to us by Your Son and our Savior, Jesus Christ. In His name we pray. Amen.

Prayer for City Council

Gracious God, on behalf of all who are gathered here today, thank You for Your abundant blessings of life and the measure of health we need to fulfill our callings. Thank You for the freedom to participate in useful work and for the honor of bearing our appropriate responsibilities. Thank You, as well for the freedom to worship You or to choose not to worship at all.

In Scriptures You have directed Your people to obey the governing authorities since You have established them to promote peace and order and justice. Therefore, we pray for our mayor, for the various levels of city officials and, in particular, for this assembled council. We ask that You would graciously grant them:

- Wisdom to govern amid the conflicting interests and issues
- A sense of the welfare for the true needs of our citizens
- A keen interest in justice and righteousness
- A confidence in what is good and appropriate
- And an ability to work together in harmony even when there's honest disagreement

We also ask Your blessing of personal peace for those on this council in their lives and joy in their service to our community.

We pray for the agenda set before them and please give them an assurance of what would please You and what would benefit those who live and work in and around our beloved city of Los Banos.

This we pray in your Son's Name, Amen.

Made in the USA
Coppell, TX
31 August 2021